BIBLE INSIGHTS: BIBLE BOOK STUDY

2 TIMOTHY
Standing Up to Pressure

By Dave Rahberg

Editor: Thomas A. Nummela

Editorial associate: Rachel C. Hoyer

We solicit your comments and suggestions concerning this material. Please write to Product Manager, Youth Bible Studies, CPH, 3558 S. Jefferson Avenue, St. Louis, MO 63118-3968.

Scripture quotations are taken from the HOLY BIBLE, NEW INTERNATIONAL VERSION®. NIV®. Copyright © 1973, 1978, 1984 by International Bible Society. Used by permission of Zondervan Publishing House. All rights reserved.

Copyright © 1996 Concordia Publishing House
3558 South Jefferson Avenue, St. Louis, MO 63118-3968
Manufactured in the United States of America.

All rights reserved. Except for the Student Pages, which the purchaser may reproduce for classroom use or for use in parish-education programs, no part of this publication may be reproduced, stored in a retrieval system, or transmitted, in any form or by any means, electronic, mechanical, photocopying, recording, or otherwise, without the prior written permission of Concordia Publishing House.

1 2 3 4 5 6 7 8 9 10   05 04 03 02 01 00 99 98 97 96

Contents

Welcome to Bible Insights!   4
Introduction to the Book of 2 Timothy   5
Study 1:   Encouragement   11
            Student Pages 1–3
Study 2:   Approval   19
            Student Pages 4–7
Study 3:   Godliness   29
            Student Pages 8–10
Study 4:   Charge!   39
            Student Pages 11–14

Welcome to *Bible Insights!*

Welcome to the Bible Insights series of Bible studies for youth! These materials are designed to provide study opportunities that explore selected books of the Bible in depth and apply the wisdom these books impart to the real-life issues young people face. Each book in this series has been carefully prepared to speak to the needs and concerns of youth, providing insight from God's Word. Each book consists of four sessions of study and can be used for weekly group Bible study, individual study, or a Bible-study retreat or seminar.

This book is designed for the leader of the sessions. It provides all the information and instructions necessary for an effective Bible study. Each study includes material you can reproduce for the students in your group. Additional information on the Bible book to be studied and some helpful information about small-group Bible studies are included in the Introduction.

May God bless your study by the Spirit's power, as you lead young people to greater insight about God's Word and the good things God desires to bring through it to their lives.

Introduction to the Book of 2 Timothy

Purpose and Theme

St. Paul was serious about his mission in life. His goal was to proclaim God's love for all people throughout the world. Yet one dream remained—to preach the Gospel in the most important city of the day. In time, Paul made his way to Rome. But his ministry there would exact a high price. When he wrote this letter, Paul was a prisoner in chains, facing execution. But his belief in Jesus Christ set him free from the cold, heavy iron shackles and stone walls. He invited Timothy, and Christians in all times and places, to continue the mission from God in response to grace received in Jesus Christ. Paul had been beaten, mocked, run out of town, and shipwrecked twice—all in pursuit of his mission to proclaim God's grace to a hostile world. Yet his eyes are focused on the crown of righteousness that God promised him because of Jesus' life, death, and resurrection.

This is the last letter that Paul sends to Timothy. He loves Timothy as a dear "son" in the faith. He encourages the young man as a father, a mentor, and a partner in the ministry. In chapter 4, as Paul summarizes his own life in God's service, he urges Timothy to carry on. Paul's life is drawing to a close; yet the Gospel must be proclaimed to the next generation. It remains for Timothy, and others whom God calls, to continue in his stead.

As students participate in the discussion of 2 Timothy, three important themes are repeated. First, as Timothy celebrates his own salvation, he is encouraged to continue growing in his personal faith in Jesus Christ. He never "graduates" from learning how to trust God in every situation. Second, as pastor of the Christian congregation, Timothy is called upon to recruit more "approved" leaders like himself, who know the love of God and live as disciples of the Lord Jesus. Third, Timothy is warned to avoid the traps and distractions that hinder his mission of proclaiming the Gospel. As they study this book, class members will recognize God's invitation to grow in faith, to use their gifts in ministry and leadership positions, and to witness to Jesus Christ as Lord and Savior. In addition, they will compare the snares Timothy faced with life today. Finally, your class will rehearse their own proclamations of faith in preparation for the opportunities the Holy Spirit will provide for them in the future.

Who Was Timothy?

It is no great surprise that this letter—perhaps the final extant letter from Paul—is addressed to Timothy, his fellow missionary, co-worker, and spiritual son. Paul had apparently first met Timothy in Lystra during the first missionary journey, proclaiming the Gospel and nurturing young Timothy in the faith. It was the beginning of more than 20 years of friendship, beginning with Paul mentoring Timothy spiritually and culminating many years later with Paul's urgent request that Timothy come to ease the rigors of a Roman prison cell.

Upon his return to Lystra on his second missionary journey, Paul recruited Timothy to travel with Silas and himself. Timothy's mother was a Jewish Christian and his father, a Greek. To facilitate Timothy's work among the Jews, Paul circumcised him before they set out, an act apparently neglected, or opposed by his father, in his infancy. Timothy spent at least the next 8 to 10 years traveling with Paul, or traveling at Paul's request as an "apostolic representative" to various Christian congregations in Macedonia, Achaia (Greece), and Asia Minor. As the third missionary journey concludes, Timothy accompanies Paul to Jerusalem, where Paul is arrested and begins his long-awaited trip to Rome. Timothy is named as co-sender of six of Paul's letters.

At the time of this last letter, Timothy has apparently been serving the congregation at Ephesus for five years or more. Whether Paul has been imprisoned for this entire time is not known, but it clear from Paul's tone that his situation is grave. Paul is confident of his approaching "crown of righteousness," but his earthly future is uncertain, and he turns to a true friend and Christian "son" and brother for comfort.

A Few Suggestions for Your Study

1. Use a variety of learning styles. Remember, everyone learns differently. Most teens learn best through experience. With that in mind, various activities are used to introduce the lesson themes.

2. The lesson plans offer some options. Each lesson contains more material than you will need. This gives you the opportunity to select activities that fit your group. Be sensitive to the needs of the young people in your class. Listen to them and respond to their needs.

3. Active learning fits the needs of contemporary youth. Young people live in a fast-paced world. Limit any activity to 15 minutes. Allow discussions to flow freely. Encourage participants to express their feelings as well as their thoughts.

4. Relax and have fun. If the young people see you putting yourself into the lesson, they will follow along. Be yourself. Talk about your faith struggles. By sharing your feelings you will give students permission to share theirs.

5. Invite the young people to bring their own Bibles for the study and to record insights about the text.

6. Occasionally, you may want everyone to use the same version of the Bible. This will help the group focus on the lesson without becoming lost in the different translations and interpretations.

7. Several times students will be asked to read aloud a section of Scripture. In those situations, ask for volunteers. However, if you must select someone, choose a capable and confident student. Never use reading the Bible as a punishment for misbehavior in class.

8. After a Bible reading, check to make sure all the students understand important words and phrases. Taking time to clarify concepts will make your class more meaningful for your students.

9. When you ask the class to complete an exercise within a given time, be sure to give a two- and then a one-minute warning before you call the class back to order.

10. If your group is larger than eight, consider working in two or more groups when the lesson calls for discussion or personal sharing.

11. Model the behaviors, the confidentiality, and the vulnerability you expect from your class. You have the position and opportunity to increase the spiritual depth of your discussion by your actions. Protect the person who risks sharing from the heart, and encourage your students to give their full attention to the words of their peers.

Building Relationships

Jesus desires to be our close friend as we take our daily walk of discipleship. It is beneficial to have Christian friends who can support us in that journey. Hopefully, this class will enable some of those relationships to develop. It begins with you.

Take time to get to know the members of your class. The most important time in any session is the 10–15 minutes before class begins. You need to be prepared to teach prior to that time. Be ready to greet the students as they arrive. Listen with interest as they talk about the things going on in their lives.

Try to spend some time outside of class with your students. Eating together is a great relationship-builder. Call them on the telephone just to talk. Remember their birthdays and recognize each special achievement with a card or note.

Strive to build relationships within the class as well. Encourage small-group discussions. Be sensitive to those who might be left on the outside. Attempt to help the others understand their situation in the hope that they will seek to include them. Do your best to promote class unity.

Teacher/Student Relationships

Our teaching may only be as strong as our relationships with our class members. As we learn to know our students—and as they learn to know us—our ability to direct our teaching to their lives and their ability to listen both improve.

Some suggestions:

• *Maintain a balance* between being the teacher and being a friend. You're not a teenager. And you don't need to be one or act like one to relate to your class. Your are, however, a potentially significant person in the lives of your students. Many young people seek adults with whom they can relate and on whom they can count.

• *Don't talk down to your students.* High school students see themselves as "no longer children." They will relate best to adults who give them credit for all their strengths and potential, and who are gentle with reminders that they have some areas in their lives in which they need to grow. Resist sarcasm, teasing, and put-downs of any kind.

- *Participate with your students* in class activities. Share your own responses as examples to the students. If you ask students to cut, paste, or draw, be a willing participant in the activity. It will quickly blunt any perception that such activities are childish.
- *Sit, if possible.* With a small group, in a single circle, or around a table, sit at the same level as your class. Stand when leading several small groups or in a situation where all the participants may not be able to see you otherwise.
- *Refrain from "teacher only" privileges.* If food or drink is not allowed for the students, finish yours before you enter the room or save it until after class. If refreshments are appropriate, make sure they are available to the entire class.

If your group is small, you may be able to participate in one of the small-group discussions during class. If more than two or three groups form, it may be wiser to "float" among the groups. Recognize that young people may filter their responses and opinions with an adult present in their small group.

Be sensitive to the feelings of your students. As you respect them, they will grow in their respect for you.

(From *Bible Impact*, Book 4, p. 73, © 1994 CPH. All rights reserved.)

Teaching without Student Pages

In response to the requests of many teachers, the Bible Insights studies are designed with Student Pages that you may duplicate. However, your class may be getting tired of a steady diet of study sheets, or perhaps you or your students simply don't like them. You may wish to omit some and use others. Or you may wish to do without them entirely. Here are some suggestions for adapting the lessons:

- Write response activities (sentence completions, multiple choice questions, or true/false statements) on the chalkboard or newsprint before class. Students can still respond and discuss in small groups or as a whole class.
- Write Bible references and discussion questions on index cards. Distribute the cards to individual students or small groups at the appropriate time.
- Adapt Student Page activities so they can be done without the sheet of paper. For example, rather than having the students mark a set of response scales on a Student Page, have them stand at imaginary points along the longest wall of your classroom. The wall becomes the scale as you read the response statements.
- You can frequently lead a class discussion from questions on the Student Page or invite small groups to discuss the questions one at a time.
- For some activities, you can have the students respond on blank paper or draw their own version of the Student Page illustration before completing the activity.

- Omit activities that are strictly paper-oriented and substitute more active ones. Even teenagers enjoy simple games and *active* learning assignments.
- If no other solution is obvious, scan the Student Page activity to determine the purpose it serves in the progression of the lesson and summarize that point directly. Or invent another method of communicating it to the students.

Evaluation

Evaluation should be a part of every session. Take time after each session to reflect on activities that went well or didn't work and why, concepts some students didn't grasp, and new issues or concerns you heard from your students.

Occasionally, take time after class to discuss with at least a few of the students the following questions: What was the best part of the class session today? If you were the teacher, what things would you do differently? What is the most important thing that you learned?

Incorporate the things you learn into your future lesson planning.

Encouragement 1

(2 Timothy 1:1–14)

Focus

The Good News of salvation through faith in Jesus Christ is a source of endless encouragement to those who suffer physical distress, temptation to sin, or spiritual trials of any kind. The apostle Paul writes his final letter to his young friend and co-worker Timothy to encourage him in his ministry. In God's Word we too can find grace, mercy, and peace—for ourselves and for sharing with others.

Objectives

That by the power of the Holy Spirit the participants will
1. identify the ways Paul encourages Timothy;
2. describe the source of Paul's confidence, his own faith in Jesus Christ;
3. develop a plan to encourage someone with the Gospel.

Materials Needed

- Your own letter of encouragement or recognition
- Newsprint, makers, and tape, or chalkboard and chalk
- Pens or pencils, stationery or blank paper, envelopes
- Bibles
- Copies of Student Pages 1–3

Lesson Outline: Encouragement

Activity	Minutes	Materials Needed
Warmup	10	Personal letter or award (optional)
Prayer	2	
Two Basic Concepts	15	Student Pages 1 & 2, Bibles, pencils, newsprint and masking tape
Personal Mission Statement	15–20	Student Page 3, pencils
Encouraging Others	10	Stationery or blank paper, envelopes, pencils
Closing Prayer	2	

Preparation

Select a letter or award to bring for the first warmup activity, if you wish, and review and complete a copy of Student Page 3.

Warmup

Choose one of the following activities.

Share an encouraging letter you have written or received with your class. A letter of recognition for accomplishments or some other award could also be used. Read the letter or show the award to the whole class and describe the impact it has had on your attitude and life ambitions. What feelings surfaced in your heart? Then invite the students to share a similar experience of their own.

Or ...

Identify a person who has made a positive impression on you in the past year. How has that individual encouraged you to be faithful to Jesus Christ? What did they do that helped you to experience God's love in a personal way? Again, allow volunteers to share similar experiences.

Present the session objectives to the class. You might consider posting them in a way and place that the students can see throughout the study session.

Prayer

Ask the class to join you in a prayer. Use or adapt the following prayer: "Gracious Father, You have given us this time together to encourage each other through Your Holy Word. Help us to claim Your mercy, love, and power for our own lives. Thank You for loving us and giving us Jesus Christ as our Savior. In His strong name we pray, Amen."

The Basic Concepts

Review the historical situation and emotional impact this letter has for us as described in the "Introduction to 2 Timothy." Highlight points that will be informative for your class. Focus on the encouragement Paul gives and the mission he describes for Timothy, even though Paul is facing his own execution. Paul sees imprisonment and death as the final step in his service to his loving God.

Also distribute Student Page 1, "Meet Timothy," and let the students review the history of Paul's relationship with Timothy. Remind the students that the dates on the time line are only approximate.

Make sure each person has a Bible. Read, or have volunteers read, **2 Timothy 1:1–14** aloud for the whole class. Encourage students to note any puzzling passages. Clarify for the class any questions about the vocabulary or historical context.

Distribute Student Page 2. Direct the students to work in pairs, or small groups, to complete the Student Page. Ask each team to copy their definitions onto newsprint and post it.

Allow for the students to work about 10 minutes. While they work, write the following sample definitions on newsprint. Invite volunteers to share their definitions. Then compare the students' definitions with the samples.

For the Christian, *encouragement* is an intentional effort that inspires someone to persevere in a challenging situation, inviting God to strengthen that individual for the task at hand.

For the Christian, a personal *mission* expresses the values and beliefs about God's will for his life on earth until God takes him to heaven. This mission can provide direction in times of decision-making.

Make a two-column chart on newsprint or the chalkboard. Label one column *encouragement* and the other *mission*. Ask each team to write its Scripture references and key words in the appropriate column.

Ask the class, "How does Paul's mission affect his feelings about his impending execution?" (He seems joyful and expectant, as if this will be the long-awaited conclusion.) Then ask, "Why is Paul able to speak so positively about his impending death?" (Paul has faith in Christ and the sure hope of eternal life.)

Personal Mission Statement

Distribute copies of Student Page 3. Review the Student Page and share your first-draft mission statement with the class. Give the students an opportunity to work on their own personal mission statements for about 15 minutes. Then invite each student to find a partner with whom they can share their mission statement. When both partners have shared, invite each one to pray for his or her partner to have the courage, wisdom, strength, and opportunity to pursue that mission.

Encouraging Others

Distribute stationery and envelopes. Ask each student to write a letter of encouragement to someone he or she knows. Each could select a quote from one of the verses in **2 Timothy 1.** In the letter, describe how this person has touched their lives with God's love. Participants do not have to share their letter with the class. Offer to mail the letters.

Closing Prayer

Close the session with a prayer. Include petitions from the group. You can adapt the following prayer: "Dear Father, You have encouraged us in Your Word. You have given us a spirit of power, love, and self-discipline. Help us to boldly celebrate Your gifts this week. *[Insert the prayer concerns of your students here.]* Thank You for Your absolute love and complete forgiveness. Bless us and give us the will to do Your work this week. In Jesus' name, Amen."

Extending the Lesson

Give each student a piece of blank paper and markers or crayons. Ask the students, "What is your most precious material possession? In what ways do you guard and protect it?" Invite them to draw that possession. After a few minutes, share your own drawing and then invite volunteers to share their drawings. (For example, the leader might say, "My most precious material possession is my car. I wash it, maintain it according to the manufacturer's specifications, keep it in my garage, and lock it whenever I leave it in a parking lot or parked on the street.") Students' responses will vary.

Then ask, "What valued possession is Paul talking about in **2 Timothy 1:12, 14**?" Most commentaries agree that Paul is speaking of the Gospel and Christian faith.

Finally ask, "How does the Holy Spirit work in us to guard our faith in the Gospel?" Through Baptism, the Holy spirit has worked saving faith in us and made us members of God's family. Daily the Spirit leads us into fellowship with other Christians, draws us to hear and study God's Word, strengthens us in our faith and life through Baptism and Holy Communion, dwells in us to guard us from temptation to do evil, and also gives us spiritual mentors—teachers, pastors, and other adults—who help us stay close to Him. Help your students identify the sources of assistance that are most prominent, or most scarce, in their own lives. Encourage them to give thanks for the spiritual help they have and to make specific plans to strengthen other such areas.

Meet Timothy

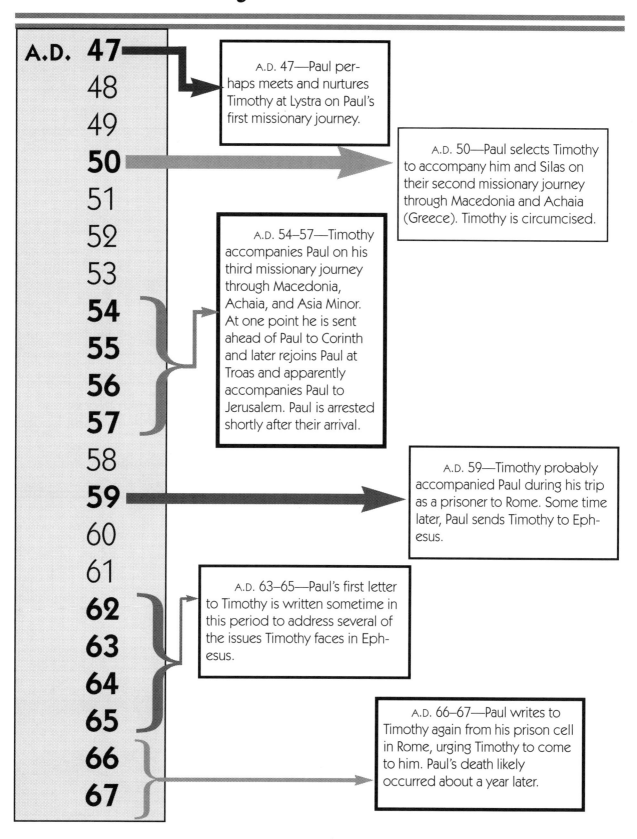

2 Timothy, Student Page 1

Two Basic Concepts

There are two important concepts in **2 Timothy 1:1–14**: *encouragement* and *mission*. How would you define these concepts? In the space below, write a brief definition of each.

Encouragement

Mission

Using your definitions, review **2 Timothy 1:1–14**. Identify three verses from this chapter that are mostly words of encouragement and three that speak of Paul's mission or the mission he sees for Timothy.

Encouragement Verses

1. 6
2. 7
3. 8

Mission Verses

1.
2. 13
3. 14

A Personal Mission Statement

> *In joyful celebration of eternal life with Jesus, I am inviting people to use their gifts, improve their abilities, and expand their vision for personal ministry.*

Developing a personal mission statement is a lifelong task. It will require knowing yourself and taking time for reflection. Use the following questions to start the process in your life.

1. What three behaviors bring you the most satisfaction?

2. What gives you a sense of value and self-worth?

3. What three adjectives describe you?

4. List three verbs that describe the way you want to live.

5. As a Christian what three benefits do you have from God?

6. Use your answers from the preceding questions to create a first draft of your own mission statement. Strive for 25 words or less. This word limit will make it easy to remember and use. See the sample on this page.

© 1996 CPH

2 Timothy, Student Page 3

Approval 2
(2 Timothy 2:11–26)

Focus

God's people are pulled in two directions. Satan and our sinful flesh pull us to seek final approval with others through godless behavior and idle words. God works in us to seek His approval in godly actions motivated and supported by the work of His Son Jesus Christ. As Christ lives in us we can flee sin and embrace God's will and approval.

Objectives

That by the power of the Holy Spirit the participants will
1. describe the unconditional approval and acceptance God gives all believers in Jesus;
2. recognize that God's approval gives Christians freedom from sin and the power to live according to God's will;
3. describe how the world benefits when God's people live in His approval.

Materials Needed

- Bibles
- Pens or pencils
- Soft foam ball
- Newsprint, markers, and masking tape
- One Band-Aid
- Blank paper
- Copies of Student Pages 4–7

Lesson Outline: Approval

Activity	Minutes	Materials
Warmup (Optional) Lesson Introduction and Prayer	5	Soft foam ball
Approved	20	Newsprint and markers, Student Page 4, Bibles, pencils, blank paper
Your Turn	10	Student Page 5, pencils
A Case in Point	10	Student Page 6
Closing Activity	5	

Warmup (Optional)

Play a short game of ball tag. In a small room a soft foam ball is best. Or you can substitute a crumpled piece of newsprint secured with a couple of strips of tape. The person last tagged with the ball is it. He or she must tag someone else by throwing the ball and hitting another person below the neck. Stop the game after five minutes or if students get out of control.

When the game is over and students are seated ask, "Which part of the game were you better at—avoiding the ball or pursuing others with it?" Allow a few volunteers to share. Then ask, "Which is more important in winning a game of tag—escape or pursuit?" (In reality they both contribute to success in the game.)

Lesson Introduction and Prayer

Introduce today's study by sharing the "Focus" and "Objectives" with the students. Consider posting the objectives where the students can see them throughout the study. Use or adapt the following prayer: "Dear Savior, we often struggle for approval. We seek to wear the right clothes, to have the right friends, and to say the right things. We want desperately to belong and are often willing to pay a great price for the approval of others. Today help us to know Your approval. May it free us to act according to Your will and to celebrate our relationship with You. Help us to know Your love and to share it joyfully with the people around us. We pray in the name of Jesus, through whom we have Your approval. Amen."

Approved

Divide the group into two teams. Give each team a sheet of newsprint and markers. Direct each team to appoint a secretary to record the results of a brainstorming session. Challenge the teams to generate a list of "things for which a young person might need approval." Examples: going out on Friday night, borrowing a parent's car. Call time in four minutes. Then ask each group to post its list and count its total number of entries.

Congratulate the team with the most entries. Ask volunteers to identify an item from the lists for which they sought approval recently. Ask each volunteer: (1) Who had to give approval? (2) On what basis was approval given or denied?

Now direct the students to **2 Timothy 2:14–26.** Read aloud the passage to the group. Direct the class to write on a sheet of paper (left column) words or phrases that represent sinful human behavior. Have students write in the right column words or phrases that describe Christlike behavior and goals. (As an alternative, they could simply write plus [+] or minus [-] in their Bibles.)

Make two columns on newsprint or the board. Record key words and verse numbers as volunteers share the verses they marked (-) and (+). The minus column could include the following: quarreling **(v. 14)**; godless chatter **(v. 16)**; ignoble purposes **(vv. 20–21)**; evil desires **(v. 22)**; arguments **(v. 23)**; quarrel, resentment **(v. 24)**; escape devil's trap **(v. 26)**. The plus column might include these verses: remind [of God's faithfulness] **(v. 14)**; present yourself as approved **(v. 15)**; pursue righteousness, etc. **(v. 22)**; be kind, teach **(v. 24)**.

Distribute Student Page 4. Allow students to work through the discussion questions in groups of two or three. After about five minutes, review the questions with the whole group. Use the following to guide your discussion.

1. "According to these verses, what approval should Timothy seek?" (Status as an able workman correctly handling the Word of truth, **v. 15**.)

2. "From whom?" (God.)

3. "What are the conditions of God's approval?" (*Not by Timothy's actions*—avoiding evil or pursuing righteousness! These things result *from* God's approval. Paul says the only "condition" is faith in the Gospel. Point students to **v. 8,** "remember Jesus Christ," and **v. 25**, "God will grant them repentance leading them to a knowledge of the truth.")

4. "What are the most 'valuable' and the least 'valuable' vessels (dishes or containers) in your home?" (Highlight **v. 21.** The vessels of gold, silver, wood, and clay can all prove to be useful to the Master's good work. There are a variety of different abilities and gifts in the Lord's house. All can be "noble" to God. In both verses, approval is not from other people. Absolute approval is granted from God Himself. Other efforts will be fruitless and are the "ignoble" vessels in the Master's house.)

5. Look at **2 Timothy 2:19.** "How does God know you are His redeemed child?" (He sees you sealed in faith and forgiveness through Baptism and chosen for eternal life in Christ.)

Your Turn

Remind the students that Timothy is a young man, perhaps in his early twenties, not much older than most class members. Point out that Timothy has been taught by Paul and serves as resident pastor of the church at Ephesus. It may be that in the not-so-distant future, one or more students in your class may have a similar calling. In any event, Paul's words are also directed by the Holy Spirit to us for our spiritual growth.

Distribute copies of Student Page 5. Invite students to work through the page in pairs or groups of three. Allow 10 minutes for their work. Then invite volunteers to share responses with the whole group. Add or emphasize the following comments during the discussion.

1. Answers will vary according to your students' experience. Accept all reasonable responses.

2. Again responses will vary. Examples might be righteousness, regular attendance at church and Bible study; faith, willingness to talk with others about spiritual matters; love, going out of your way to help someone in need; peace, displaying an attitude of contentment and calmness in the midst of a hectic world.

3. Students might emphasize either one. Ideally, both will be present in the lives of Christians. In one way, it may be easier to "flee" unrighteousness if we are purposefully pursuing righteous behavior under the influence of Christ at work in us.

4. Each individual's effectiveness will vary; do not expect or push for volunteers here. Focus on the second question. God's approach will be most difficult when emotions get in the way.

5. We are saved, not because of our works, but by the grace of God. Works are a response to God's generous love, and His will is for us to bring people into His kingdom. The Holy Spirit uses our works to open the hearts of other people for the Gospel.

A Case in Point

Choose two volunteers for a roleplay. Adapt the situation to a case study if you have a shy group.

Give each volunteer a section of Student Page 6 with a basic story line and character to present during the roleplay. Ask them to read it and prepare while you introduce the scene to the class.

Use the following statement to prepare the class for the roleplay. "This is Mr. (Mrs.) Tim. He [or she] boldly witnesses to his [her] faith in Jesus as Lord and Savior. He is also a committed Sunday school teacher who wants everyone to know God's love in Christ. Today Mr. (Mrs.) Tim has visitors in his Sunday morning class. These three individuals have very different convictions about God and Christian faith. Let's watch their interaction. Pay attention to strong points each character makes."

Invite the class to note when Mr. Tim is most effective in his witness and when he faces difficult challenges from the visitors. Direct the players to begin. Allow the roleplay to continue until there is no further progress. Ask the whole class to comment. Invite the class to suggest ways to make the Sunday school teacher's witness more effective. List them on the board or on newsprint.

Ask, "Did Mr. (Mrs.) Tim employ the advice Paul gave Timothy? **(2 Timothy 2:24–25)** How did or could Paul's advice help?"

Closing Activity

Ask people to find a partner to pray with today. They need to find someone they trust and move next to that person. In their pairs, ask them to respond to the following questions. This week who is most likely to "quarrel" with you? How could you turn the situation around into God "approved" response? After both have finished answering the question, pray for the other person. When they are finished praying, the students may quietly leave the room, or quietly wait to be dismissed.

Extending the Lesson

Direct the students to the early verses in this chapter—**2 Timothy 2:1–10.** Remind them that "approval"—our justification—comes from

God through the work of Jesus Christ without any merit or good works on our part. Yet Paul uses three vivid personnel pictures to convey some truth about our relationship to God. Divide the students into three groups. Assign each group one of the roles of (1) soldier, **verses 3–4;** (2) athlete, **verse 5;** or (3) farmer, **verse 6.** Encourage the groups to study their verse or verses in the context of the entire chapter and in several different translations if possible. Ask them to prepare a simple report on their assigned role that completes the following two sentence stems:

Our Christian life is like that of a [soldier, athlete, or farmer] because …

Knowing we are already approved—justified by God through Christ—helps us to fulfill this role by …

Distribute copies of the optional Student Page 7, or provide newsprint on which they can write their responses. After a few moments, allow each group to share its work. Affirm and comment on their responses based on these samples:

Our Christian life is like that of a **soldier** because *we are called into and empowered by the Spirit for a life of service, gladly doing the will of our commanding officer.* Knowing we are already approved—justified by God through Christ—helps us to fulfill this role by *strengthening faith and assuring us of our forgiveness and the certain hope of eternal life.*

Our Christian life is like that of an **athlete** because *we know and adhere to the "rules" of Christian living, by God's grace and with His power.* Knowing we are already approved—justified by God through Christ—helps us to fulfill this role by *strengthening our faith and assuring us of forgiveness and the certain hope of eternal life—our crown of victory.*

Our Christian life is like that of a **farmer** because *we share in the blessings God provides, especially the spiritual fruit of love, joy, peace … (See Galatians 5:22–23).* Knowing we are already approved—justified by God through Christ—helps us to fulfill this role by *strengthening our faith and assuring us of forgiveness and the certain hope of eternal life.*

Approved

Paul addresses several items of critical importance to his young friend and "student minister" Timothy. One of them is the matter of approval. Based on **2 Timothy 2:11–26,** respond to the following questions.

1. What approval is Timothy encouraged to seek?

2. From whom?

3. What are the conditions of approval?

4. Think about the most valuable and least valuable "vessels"—plates, cups, and the like—in your house. They are all useful for the purpose for which plates and cups were made. According to Paul, is God more concerned with *noble condition* or with *noble purpose?* What meaning should this illustration have for Timothy?

5. How does "the Lord [know] those who are His" (verse 19)?

2 Timothy, Student Page 4   Scripture quotations: NIV®. © 1996 CPH

Your Turn

Paul understands how much Timothy is seeking approval. The young pastor is torn between serving God and pleasing the people in his congregation. Paul's letter is going to help Timothy sort out his priorities. Those priorities are important principals for our Christian lives today.

1. Paul tells Timothy to flee from the "evil desires of youth." List three things which keep today's young people from living in ways God would approve.

2. Paul tells Timothy to pursue four behaviors in his desire to have God's approval. Give one example of each of these behaviors for youth today:

    Righteousness —

    Faith —

    Love —

    Peace —

3. Paul encourages Timothy to run away from youthful desires that gratify his sinful flesh and chase after righteousness, faith, love, and peace like all the other faithful believers. Which are you doing more of today, running away from or chasing?

4. Check **2 Timothy 2:24–26.** Gentle, patient teaching expresses the hope that eventually God will lead the other person to salvation. How effective are you when you use this approach? When is a Christian going to have the greatest difficulty using God's approach?

5. Read **Ephesians 2:4–10.** What reminder does Paul give here about our actions? Whom do our actions benefit?

© 1996 CPH   Scripture quotations: NIV®.

A Case in Point

Mr. [Mrs.] Tim. You are a Sunday school teacher at All Saints Worship Center. You are a bold witness to Jesus as your Lord and Savior, and you have a desire to share God's love with all people. Today you have visitors in class who present challenges to your convictions. As you listen to their comments, share your faith, through Bible passages and/or doctrinal truths, in Jesus Christ as the only way to God's full and free salvation.

Visitor 1. You believe the advice of your parents, "God helps those who help themselves." You believe that it is what we do that matters, not what we think or feel or say. You have worked hard at home, school, and sports, and you believe that you will succeed in life and please God by your best efforts and determination.

Visitor 2. You believe that all religions are basically the same. There is one universal truth that is available to everyone and all we need is more patience, tolerance, and respect toward one another. In the end, God accepts all people as long as they are sincere.

Visitor 3. You believe that God would never punish anyone. Though some people may turn out "bad," God will ultimately welcome everyone into heaven.

2 Timothy, Student Page 6 © 1996 CPH

Personnel Pictures

Soldier

Endure hardship with us like a good soldier of Christ Jesus. No one serving as a soldier gets involved in civilian affairs—he wants to please his commanding officer. 2 Timothy 2:3–4

Athlete

Similarly, if anyone competes as an athlete, he does not receive the victor's crown unless he competes according to the rules. 2 Timothy 2:5

Farmer

The hardworking farmer should be the first to receive a share of the crops. 2 Timothy 2:6

Our Christian life is like that of a [soldier, athlete, or farmer] because ...

Knowing we are already approved—justified by God through Christ—helps us to fulfill this role by ...

© 1996 CPH   Scripture quotations: NIV®.   **2 Timothy, Student Page 7**

Godliness
(2 Timothy 3:1–13)

Focus

Jesus Christ has rescued us—from the eternal death that faces those without Christ at the end of time, and from the assaults of the devil that we face in these last days before the end. God does not spare us the trials of this life, but He provides guidance and strength to stand firm in godliness.

Objectives

That by the power of the Holy Spirit, the participants will
1. recognize in Paul's description of human behaviors in the last days the realities of life today;
2. discover the power God provides against the *form of godliness* and the false teachers;
3. rejoice in the Good News that we hear through the teachings of Paul;
4. implore God's help to bring someone they know to see His love and salvation.

Materials Needed

- Bibles
- Pens or pencils for each student
- Newsprint, makers, and masking tape
- Copies of Student Pages 8–10 for each student

Lesson Outline: Love

Activity	Minutes	Materials Needed
Warmup	10	Two identical newspapers; *and* newsprint and markers
Godlessness	20	two copies of Student Page 8 for each student, pencils
Imposters	10	Copies of Student Page 9, pencils, Bibles
Your Turn	10	Copies of Student Page 10, pencils
Closing	5	

Preparation

This session offers the option of exploring the dangers to Christians of various cults and non-Christian religions. To assist you, some additional resources are listed at the end of the study. You may wish to consult this information early in your preparation to allow time to locate or order desired resources.

The information can be used to (1) expand your personal knowledge, (2) inform in-class student research and discussion, (3) serve as information for the students to take home at the end of the study, or (4) be the basis for research-and-report assignments before or after this session.

Warmup

Choose one of the following activities to begin your session.

Bring two or more copies of the same newspaper's front page. Divide the class into two teams. Give each team a sheet of blank newsprint or large paper and a marker. Give each team the newspaper page. Challenge each to identify and record as many sinful actions or attitudes as possible.

Or ...

Play Charades. Divide into teams. Act out behaviors that are opposites, such as *boastful* and humble, *abusive* and protective, *ungrateful* and thankful, *unholy* and devoted, *brutal* and kind, *disobedient* and obedient. Include other behaviors if you wish. (The negative behaviors are some of those Paul lists in **2 Timothy 3:2–4**.) Challenge those observing to guess the behavior and its opposite. Stop after a few rounds.

In either case, point out to the students that our world is full of ungodly behavior. Yet God calls us to behave differently. "In our study today we will discover how that is possible."

Review the "Focus" and "Objectives" with the class. Consider posting the objectives where students can see and review them during class.

Opening Prayer

Lead the students in a prayer such as the following: "Dear Heavenly Father, we live in a sin-plagued world. The people around us—and we ourselves—do the very things You forbid and avoid those things You command. We are sorry for our sin and seek to live differently. Be with us as we study Your Word. Create in us the will and the power to be Your people in the world, through Jesus Christ, our Lord. Amen."

Godlessness

Make copies of Student Page 8. Distribute one copy to each class member. As a group, read aloud, or ask a volunteer to read aloud, **2 Timothy 3:1–5.**

Direct students' attention to the "T-Charts" on the page. The T-chart is a tool for identifying and describing speech and actions associated with various words or concepts. The first category, "Sounds Like," helps students reflect on how their conversations and statements *embody* abstract concepts (e.g., love, patience, etc.). The second category, "Looks Like," helps students understand how their actions *personify* concepts.

As time permits, demonstrate a sample T-chart for the class. (Draw a large T-chart on the board or newsprint; as an option, use poster paper). Suggest that the class think about the word *happiness.* Ask, "What does happiness sound like?" Invite students to answer aloud. Happiness may sound like Christmas songs, the final school bell, "thank you" from a friend, "I appreciate you" from a parent. Similarly, ask students, "What does happiness look like?" Accept and encourage student responses; appropriate answers will be joyful actions.

Invite students to form small groups. Ask each group to choose four of the words or phrases describing sin from **2 Timothy 3** and complete the T-charts on the page. Encourage students to write down two or more "concrete" expressions and actions for each word or phrase. When the groups finish, bring the class together to discuss their answers.

After students share their responses, ask students to read **Galatians 5:22–23** and **Colossians 3:12–15.** Say, "Our sinful nature leads us to speak and act as though God is not important in our lives. We sin against God and against other people in our thoughts, words, and deeds. In Christ, God the Father forgives us. He declares us 'not guilty' because of the death and resurrection of Jesus for our salvation. We are baptized into Christ, and we are renewed by His mercy and strength. He is always with us to empower us to live as faithful, forgiven people."

Invite students to work again in their groups to choose one of the Spirit's fruit that opposes each of the sins they chose from **2 Timothy 3.** Again, ask students to describe or illustrate what the fruit "sounds like" and "looks like" using the back of the Student page. Gather the class together for discussion and reflection on the following questions:

1. Where does sin come from? (Our fallen nature and outside temptations.)

2. How do we obtain the fruit of the Spirit? (They are God's gifts to those who have faith in Jesus Christ.)

3. How can our lives reflect more of the *fruit* and less of *sin?* (God is at work in our lives through Word and Sacrament to strengthen our faith and increase our ability to do His will.)

Imposters!

Distribute Student Page 9. Once again invite a volunteer to read aloud, or read aloud yourself, the Scripture passage on the page. Invite students to form small discussion groups, or if class size permits, work through the questions as a group. Expand on the student responses with the following comments.

1. Paul's characterization of the imposters—false teachers—is vivid. They prey on helpless women and, it seems, people who are troubled by guilt and are searching for peace. The imposters seek to prevent others from hearing God's Word of love and forgiveness. They feed such men or

women a false peace or comfort that does not focus on God's love for us in Jesus Christ. In the end, the "weak-willed" person continues to look to false teachers for true peace. Both are at risk of eternal condemnation. The imposters also oppose God's servants—true teachers of the faith.

2. Answers will vary, but may include that the imposters kindled dissension, division, or perhaps hatred in the congregation. They certainly tried to promote their false teachings, but in addition may have wanted to entice members to leave the congregation to form a sect.

3. Point out to the class that many cult groups or occult activities fit this description. Examples could include Mormonism, Jehovah's Witnesses, horoscopes, New Age movement, fortunetellers, etc.

4. You can review the persecution Paul suffered in Antioch, Iconium, and Lystra by reading **Acts 13:45–14:19.** It might be helpful to identify the locations for the cities on a map. Point out to the students that the sufferings Paul endured in his early ministry made a lasting impression on him, especially as he recalls God's deliverance for the sake of the Gospel. These experiences of God's deliverance were an anchor during the rough times, especially now as Paul is in prison and faces execution. Throughout his career as an evangelist, Paul had never been abandoned by God.

5. Persecution today can serve a similar function. Paul explains that the Christian who lives the lifestyle God approves will be different from the world. He or she will be different enough to be noticed by people whose consciences burden them with guilt. Persecution is the unbelievers' direct response to the disapproval they sense in their own hearts. Their consciences are convicting them of their sin. By making the Christian feel some of the same pain and misery suffered now in their own sinful hearts, the unbeliever hopes to draw the Christian away from God's love and into the same snare of hopelessness. Paul describes how the unbelievers simply make their situation worse before God through their abuse of Christians. In an odd way, the persecution is a sign of God's presence in the believer's heart. Jesus discussed the same issue with the disciples in **John 16:1–4.**

6. In **2 Timothy 3:9,** Paul says that the false teachers will be exposed to everyone. The false teachers will not be totally successful. They cannot win in the end. Christ will expose their folly on Judgment Day.

Your Turn

Distribute copies of the case studies on Student Page 10. Assign one of the two studies to every two or three students in class. This same group might also work together for the closing activity. Allow the students about 10 minutes to read and discuss the issue you have assigned. Then invite a volunteer to describe each situation and the group's response. Ask other groups with that case to comment on the situation as well.

Both of the case studies are reasonably ambiguous. There could be valid arguments for or against. The principles that surface may include: (1) don't compromise your own faith, (2) be open and honest about your own beliefs and intentions in the relationships, and (3) whether they would have gone to the dance or continued the relationship, encourage the students to keep their nonchristian friends in their prayers.

Closing Activity

Direct the students back into their groups of two or three. Ask each group to discuss one or both of the following topics and spend time in prayer for one another—aloud or silently as each group chooses. Give a time limit of five minutes or so, and ask students to wait quietly for dismissal or leave the room quietly when they are done.

1. Identify one or more of the behaviors Paul describes in **2 Timothy 3:2–4,** Student Page 6, that "worm" their way into your heart and life most easily.

2. Identify a friend who is trapped, learning everything but the truth. How can you help him or her hear the Gospel this week?

Extending the Lesson

It seems that every few years a new cult or religious view gains popularity or notoriety in our world. The People's Temple in Jonestown, the New Age movement, and the followers of David Koresh in Waco are some examples that have gained national attention. Perhaps there are similar groups that are more local or familiar to your students. Take a little time to become familiar with the main teachings of such a group. Review them with your students. Then ask, "Suppose you were approached to become a participant in such a group. How might you respond? How would you explain the differences between your Christian faith and the group's teachings? What might be the weak spots or dissatisfactions in your personal life and relationship to your church that would make you vulnerable to such an approach? How can our church best support our members against such groups?"

Resources on Cults and Other Religions

As you and your students discuss various cults and non-Christian religions, you may feel the need for additional material for personal study, class discussion, research assignments, or future study. The following resources are available to assist you. They are all available from Concordia Publishing House, 3558 South Jefferson Avenue, St. Louis, MO 63118, 1-800-325-3040.

Religious Myth: The New Age, a full-color tract sold in packages of 25 for $3.99. Order number 10-1683.

The *How to Respond* series, newly updated and expanded, these 60–64 page books provide substantial information and listings of additional resources for $3.99 a book.

The Cults ....Order number 12-6001
The Lodge ....Order number 12-6003
Jehovah's Witnesses ....Order number 12-6005

The Latter-day Saints	Order number 12-6006
Muslims	Order number 12-6010
Satanism	Order number 12-6011
The New Age Movement	Order number 12-6012
Judaism	Order number 12-6013

The *You Can Know* series provides six-page, two-color brochures that describe the group and its beliefs and suggest ways to witness. Each brochure can be ordered in packages of 100 for $14.99.

Jehovah's Witnesses	Order number 092471
Mormons	Order number 092472
The Way International	Order number 092473
The Unification Church (Moonies)	Order number 092474
Hare Krishna	Order number 092475
Unity	Order number 092476
New Age Movement	Order number 092521
Worldwide Church of God	Order number 092522
The Occult	Order number 092523
Astrology	Order number 092578
Satanism	Order number 092579
Pornography	Order number 092580

Godlessness

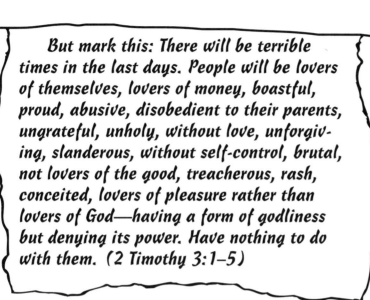

But mark this: There will be terrible times in the last days. People will be lovers of themselves, lovers of money, boastful, proud, abusive, disobedient to their parents, ungrateful, unholy, without love, unforgiving, slanderous, without self-control, brutal, not lovers of the good, treacherous, rash, conceited, lovers of pleasure rather than lovers of God—having a form of godliness but denying its power. Have nothing to do with them. (2 Timothy 3:1–5)

A "T-chart" can help to illustrate biblical words and ideas. Use the charts below to list different ways that "godlessness" is expressed in words ("Sounds Like") or actions ("Looks Like").

Sounds Like	Looks Like

Imposters!

> They [the godless] are the kind who worm their way into homes and gain control over weak-willed women, who are loaded down with sins and are swayed by all kinds of evil desires, always learning but never able to acknowledge the truth. Just as Jannes and Jambres opposed Moses, so also these men oppose the truth—men of depraved minds, who, as far as the faith is concerned, are rejected. But they will not get very far because, as in the case of those men, their folly will be clear to everyone.
>
> You, however, know all about my teaching, my way of life, my purpose, faith, patience, love, endurance, persecutions, sufferings—what kinds of things happened to me in Antioch, Iconium and Lystra, the persecutions I endured. Yet the Lord rescued me from all of them. In fact, everyone who wants to live a godly life in Christ Jesus will be persecuted, while evil men and impostors will go from bad to worse, deceiving and being deceived.
> (2 Timothy 3:6–13)

Again consider Paul's words to Timothy and respond to the questions that follow.

1. How does Paul characterize the opposition Timothy will face?

2. How might Paul phrase "weak-willed women" today?

3. What are some groups of opposition that oppose God's truth today and distract people from hearing God's love and living in a relationship with Jesus Christ?

4. Paul is trying to encourage Timothy to be a faithful minister, why does he mention his past mistreatment for the sake of Jesus? What hope is there for Timothy and Christians today in **2 Timothy 3:12?**

5. Where is Paul's encouragement to Timothy in this section?

Your Turn

This is an opportunity to put your faith to work. There are two case studies on this page. With a partner or small group read the assigned situation. Identify workable alternative solutions to each situation and select your best options. You will be invited to share your results with the whole group.

Situation 1: Your Friend, the Mormon

You have a new friend at school who is a member of a religious group that you have been told is not Christian. Your friend is a Mormon. This person sits next to you in the class right before you both have lunch, and you frequently eat together. Religion has been a topic of discussion before today, and you have both agreed to disagree. Recently, your friend went with you to one of your church youth group's social events. Now your friend has invited you to participate in a Mormon youth group dance on Friday night. It is a good chance to meet some new people. Who knows, you might even be lucky enough to get a date. When you ask your parents about going to the dance, they express some concern about being involved in a Mormon activities. Their questions include "What will happen next? Will we soon have 'missionaries' knocking at our door?" What are your options in this situation, and which one is your best choice?

Situation 2: Missionary Dating

That *perfect* person is calling you on the phone. Friends at school think this is a great match. Your social status has *definitely* improved. This special relationship does not include anything to do with church. You have invited, but you were doubtful because the conversations you've had with this special friend reveal an understanding that religion is something only weak people need.

Your parents are disappointed that you are spending time with someone who does not know Jesus Christ as their Savior. Even you have some concerns about this part of your new relationship. What are the risks for you? What are your options in this situation, and which one is your best choice?

© 1996 CPH

Charge! 4
(2 Timothy 3:10–4:8)

Focus

Our gracious God forgives us and gives us new life through His Son Jesus Christ, arms us with His powerful Word, and sends us into the world to be His agents. Throughout the persecution, hardship, and disappointment we may encounter in His service, He guards our faith and assures us of an eternity in heaven.

Objectives

By the power of the Holy Spirit, the participants will
1. list three purposes for God's Word that Paul suggests to Timothy;
2. describe Timothy's charge from Paul and apply it to their own life of faith;
3. respond to the promised *crown of righteousness* with thankful hearts and faithful service.

Materials Needed

- Bibles
- Pens or pencils
- Newsprint, makers, and masking tape
- Copies of student Pages 11–14

Lesson Outline: Charge!

Activity	Minutes	Materials Needed
Warmup	10	
A Most Useful Book	15	Student Page 11, pencils, Bibles
Timothy and God's Word	10	Student Page 12, pencils, Bibles
God's Word to Me	10	Student Page 13, pencils
Extra Practice	(Optional)	Student Pages 14 A and B
Closing Activity	10	Newsprint and markers

Warmup

Select one of the following activities.

Tell your students that you are going to have a verbal relay race. Indicate a course that your race will take from student to student (around the table or from left to right, for example). When one lap is complete, you will start over. The race involves completing the following sentence in a new way in five seconds or less: "The Bible is good for many things, but I wouldn't try to use it to …" If a student cannot invent a new completion for the sentence in the required time, he or she must say, "I pass" on the current lap and all other laps. Start the game yourself with a sample completion like, "The Bible is good for many things, but I wouldn't try to use to it to *stop a charging lion.*" Play the game until only one *runner* remains or until enthusiasm starts to wane.

Or …

Ask the students, "What is the most important task or most valuable thing you are or have been 'in charge of' at home, in school, or on a part-time job?" Affirm each response. Encourage everyone to share at least one thing.

Then, share the session focus and objectives with the students. Consider posting the objectives where they will be visible to the students throughout the study.

Lead the students in a prayer like this one: "Dear Lord, strengthen us daily by Your Word for the race we run against temptation to sin. Keep us mindful of the *crown of righteousness* that Your Son Jesus has already won for us. In His name we pray. Amen."

A Most Useful Book

If you used the first warmup activity, congratulate all the students on their creative responses. Assure them that the Bible *is* good for many things. Paul describes its primary purpose in this last letter to Timothy. Read aloud, or ask a student to read aloud, **2 Timothy 3:10–17.**

Distribute copies of Student Page 11. Direct the students to work in pairs or groups of three to complete it. After about 10 minutes, invite volunteers to share responses. Add the following comments as needed.

V. 14. Timothy has learned the Good News of Christ and the content of the Holy Scriptures first from his family, Lois and Eunice, and later from others, especially Paul.

V. 15. God's Word will make us "wise for salvation through faith in Christ Jesus."

V. 16. *God-breathed*—the whole Bible is the inspired Word of God. God wrote His Word by placing it in the minds of the writers, using their intelligence, reasoning, and resources to produce a series of books which plainly show the writers' personalities, and yet are word for word the product of God Himself. They are therefore trustworthy and true, of greater importance and worth than any human writings.

The four things are *teaching, rebuking, correcting,* and *training in righteousness.* Teaching could be described as communicating God's clear, simple, and eternal truths revealed in His Word, especially the Good News about Jesus **(John 3:16).** Rebuking is the exposure of sin and false teaching **(Galatians 1:6–8).** Correcting is gently bringing Christians back, by the authority of the Word, to God's truth and design for life **(Romans 6:4).** Training in righteousness is the ongoing devotional process by which a person grows in faith and discipleship **(Galatians 5:22–25).** They are all part of the spiritual treasures—Word and Sacrament—through which God keeps us close to Him and daily strengthens our faith.

V. 17. The third purpose Paul suggests is so that the people of God can be "thoroughly equipped for every good work." Equipped for good works implies more than just knowledge of Christ's Word. It means that God also gives us the *will and power to do* what He desires, as He tells us in **Galatians 2:20–21.**

Timothy and God's Word

Distribute copies of Student Page 12. Again direct the students to work in pairs or groups of three to complete it. After about 10 minutes, invite volunteers to share responses. Add the following comments as needed. Ask someone to read aloud **2 Timothy 4:1–8** to the class.

Vv. 1–2. Paul establishes God and Christ as witnesses to what he tells Timothy. He also sets this charge in the context of Christ's present and eternal kingdom. Timothy's charge has eternal significance.

V. 3. Don't wait until the time is ripe. It makes no difference whether the time seems appropriate. Timothy's task is to witness to the Gospel in every situation.

Vv. 4–5. Their impatience with hearing about Jesus' life, death, and resurrection as God's gracious gift of forgiveness and eternal life, is nothing new in human history. They will continue to search and never be satisfied apart from knowing Jesus Christ.

Vv. 6–9. Paul can see past his coming execution and claim the gift of eternal life because of God's gift to him in Jesus. This same gift is available to everyone who believes in Jesus Christ.

God's Word to Me

Distribute copies of Student Page 13. Direct the students to complete the page individually and silently. Tell the students that they will not be required to share their responses, but that volunteer responses will be accepted. Allow about seven minutes. Then invite comments. Review the questions briefly, adding these comments.

1. Your students may have a variety of experience—some baptized as infants and enrolled in Sunday school from an early age. Others may be new to the faith. Affirm both. Recognize that in many families, religious instruction, even faith conversations, may not be happening. Encourage students to thank those who have nurtured them in some specific way.

2. The students' spiritual needs will vary and are of a personal nature. Don't force sharing, but ask in a general way, "Which of these do you think most young people would identify as their primary need?"

3. Be bold about suggesting that some of the students in your class may be church workers some day. But more important, affirm that each of them will be used by God in important ways.

4. Affirm that God through the Gospel provides the power for us to keep our heads and "endure" in the tasks to which He calls us.

Extra Practice

If you have time, distribute copies of Student Pages 14 A and B. You can discuss one or more of the situations as case studies, or you could select one of the situations to roleplay. Ask for someone to be the Christian helper and the other person to be the person seeking God's presence. Allow people to move in and out of the Christian helper role. The unbeliever will need to be someone who can challenge, but not frustrate, your students. This could be your role as you give each participant the opportunity to respond with their witness to Jesus Christ. Allowing young people to articulate their faith in nonthreatening situations is an important step in their spiritual development.

Closing Activity

Paul's message to Timothy is spiritual encouragement and support for Timothy's ministry. "Hang in there. You have God on your side." Those can be important words for young people to hear—and to share with others. Encourage young people to identify one person who has nourished them in the faith. Or perhaps they can identify a friend who needs encouragement. Invite each student to pray for, and communicate with, that person. Allow time for each student to develop a plan to make contact—a letter, a visit, a phone call, or some other means.

Then close the session with a prayer. If you lead the class in prayer, include a time of silence during which students can prayer for the person they have identified. If students pray with and for partners, encourage them to include this person in their prayer.

Extending the Lesson

Provide the following background information to your students: "Paul's second letter to Timothy may have been the very last letter he wrote. It was apparently written from prison in Rome. Some time after its writing, perhaps just a short time later, Paul was executed for His faith and the chaos his preaching caused throughout the Roman Empire. It is a sort of 'last will and testament' of an incredible man of God. There are indications that while Paul was under house arrest earlier in his stay in Rome, now he is in much more severe conditions, perhaps chained in a prison cell, wishing for the warmth of his cloak and the greater warmth of his friends."

Direct the students—individually, in pairs, or in small groups—to review the four chapters of this prison epistle with this context in mind. Challenge them to identify at least three of the things that Paul says to Timothy that take on new or greater importance in the light of being Paul's "last words." After allowing time for their work, invite volunteers to share their insights. A few of the possibilities are noted here; there are many others.

1:4, 8, and 12: Paul may have been chained, depressed, and lonely. But he is not intimidated or willing to back down from his strong proclamation of the Christian Gospel.

1:15–18; 4:9–22: Paul is frank about those for whom his imprisonment has been an occasion for service and those in whom it has provoked fear and desertion. Still he shows mercy **(4:16)** for them.

3:10–13; 4:6–8, 18: Paul's confidence in face of execution is remarkable. Despite the hardships he has experienced and survived by God's grace—indeed, *because* of them—he is certain that Jesus will provide the final rescue and crown of righteousness for which he longs.

A Most Useful Book

V. 14. What did Timothy learn from the Scriptures? From whom did he learn? (See **2 Timothy 1:5, 13; 2:2, 8**)

V. 15. Paul points to *a first purpose for God's Word* here. It is

V. 16. Paul calls the Scriptures "God-breathed." What does this term mean? What importance does this have?

Paul gives *a second purpose for Scripture* when he says it is useful for four things:
(1) _____,
(2) _____,
(3) _____,
(4) _____.
How are these four insights different from each other? In what way are they related?

V. 17. Paul suggests yet *a third purpose for Scripture:*

What is implied in the words *thoroughly equipped for?*

---

[14] But as for you, continue in what you have learned and have become convinced of, because you know those from whom you learned it,

[15] and how from infancy you have known the holy Scriptures, which are able to make you wise for salvation through faith in Christ Jesus.

[16] All Scripture is God-breathed and is useful for teaching, rebuking, correcting and training in righteousness,

[17] so that the man of God may be thoroughly equipped for every good work.
(2 Timothy 3:14–17)

2 Timothy, Student Page 11 — Scripture quotations: NIV®. © 1996 CPH

Timothy and God's Word

[1] In the presence of God and of Christ Jesus, who will judge the living and the dead, and in view of His appearing and His kingdom, I give you this charge:

[2] Preach the Word; be prepared in season and out of season; correct, rebuke and encourage—with great patience and careful instruction.

[3] For the time will come when men will not put up with sound doctrine. Instead, to suit their own desires, they will gather around them a great number of teachers to say what their itching ears want to hear.

[4] They will turn their ears away from the truth and turn aside to myths.

[5] But you, keep your head in all situations, endure hardship, do the work of an evangelist, discharge all the duties of your ministry.

[6] For I am already being poured out like a drink offering, and the time has come for my departure.

[7] I have fought the good fight, I have finished the race, I have kept the faith.

[8] Now there is in store for me the crown of righteousness, which the Lord, the righteous Judge, will award to me on that day—and not only to me, but also to all who have longed for His appearing.
(2 Timothy 4:1–8)

Vv. 1–2. How important does Paul's charge to Timothy appear to be? How do you know?

V. 3. When Paul tells Timothy to preach in season and out of season, what does he mean?

Vv. 4–5. What are "itching ears"? Do you know people with "itching ears"? What are they looking for today?

Vv. 6–8. How is Paul encouraging Timothy?

God's Word to Me

1. I first became acquainted with God's Word …

   Those who taught me are …

2. I would benefit most from the Bible today by …

3. I may not be called to be a church worker, but I can use God's Word to help others by …

4. I expect to be able to "keep [my] head" and "endure" even when people do not respond positively to God's Word, because …

2 Timothy, Student Page 13 Scripture quotations: NIV®. © 1996 CPH

Extra Practice

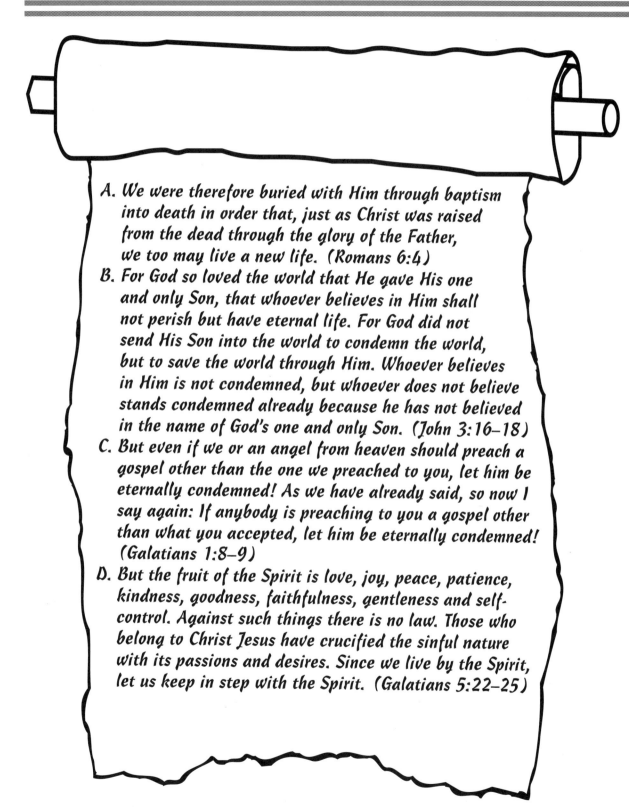

A. We were therefore buried with Him through baptism into death in order that, just as Christ was raised from the dead through the glory of the Father, we too may live a new life. (Romans 6:4)

B. For God so loved the world that He gave His one and only Son, that whoever believes in Him shall not perish but have eternal life. For God did not send His Son into the world to condemn the world, but to save the world through Him. Whoever believes in Him is not condemned, but whoever does not believe stands condemned already because he has not believed in the name of God's one and only Son. (John 3:16–18)

C. But even if we or an angel from heaven should preach a gospel other than the one we preached to you, let him be eternally condemned! As we have already said, so now I say again: If anybody is preaching to you a gospel other than what you accepted, let him be eternally condemned! (Galatians 1:8–9)

D. But the fruit of the Spirit is love, joy, peace, patience, kindness, goodness, faithfulness, gentleness and self-control. Against such things there is no law. Those who belong to Christ Jesus have crucified the sinful nature with its passions and desires. Since we live by the Spirit, let us keep in step with the Spirit. (Galatians 5:22–25)

Extra Practice—continued

Read the passages on page 14A and describe how you might use God's Word in the following situations.

1. Sally has been worshiping with you for a long time. Jesus has been her Savior since her Baptism. She wants to know how to change some behaviors that she knows are wrong. Sally confides that she has been shoplifting lately. How can she benefit from God's Word today?

2. PJ asks you to join him for a bicycle hike on Sunday. This has been something you have been hoping would happen. But of all the days to ask you! This Sunday you are involved in the youth musical at church. When you awkwardly express your regrets to PJ, he says he would like to see the musical. He has never been to church. How can he benefit from God's Word today?

3. Althea has made a terrible mistake. She is not married, but she is pregnant. She is embarrassed and *scared*. She would like to avoid the whole thing and doesn't know what to do. She has asked God for His forgiveness and wants to know His will. The baby's father does not know about God's love for His people. Althea has some important decisions to make right now. How can she benefit from God's Word today?

4. John has found something new. A call to "The Psychic Hotline" (a 1-900 number) has provided him with some really helpful advice about selecting a career and a college. At Bible class, he was excited to share his discoveries. He has shared the phone number and wants you to call, too, so you can find out the same information for yourself. How can John benefit from God's Word today?

2 Timothy, Student Page 14B

© 1996 CPH